Toys and Models

Ruth Thomson

Photography by Neil Thomson

SEA-TO-SEA

Mankato Collingwood London

This edition first published in 2010 by
Sea-to-Sea Publications
Distributed by Black Rabbit Books
P.O. Box 3263
Mankato, Minnesota 56002

Copyright © Sea-to-Sea Publications 2010

Printed in USA

9 8 7 6 5 4 3 2

Published by arrangement with the Watts
  Publishing Group Ltd., London.

Library of Congress Cataloging-in-Publication Data

Thomson, Ruth, 1949-
  Toys and models / Ruth Thomson ; photography by
Neil Thomson.
      p. cm. -- (World of design)
  Includes bibliographical references and index.
  ISBN 978-1-59771-209-5 (hardcover : alk. paper)
 1. Toy making--Juvenile literature. 2. Handicraft--Juvenile
literature. I. Thomson, Neil, 1948 Aug. 8- II. Title.
  TT174.T68 2010
  745.592--dc22
                                    2008043868

Design: Rachel Hamdi and Holly Fulbrook
Editor: Anne Civardi

The author would like to thank Islington Education Library
Service (www.objectlessons.org) and Lisa Wood for the loan of
items from their collections.

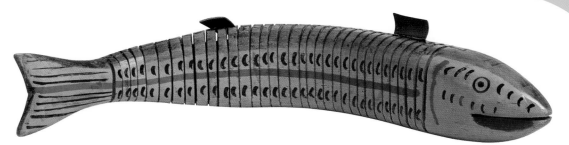

Contents

Painted wooden stacking dolls from Russia

A jute doll and boat from Bangladesh

Toy making

People everywhere make toys and models to amuse children. Their designs are often inspired by the people, animals, and traditions in the place where they live.

Notice that the Mexican clay leopard below has a hollow in its back. It is a copy of an Aztec altar from hundreds of years ago. The stacking dolls are painted with shawls and embroidered clothes, similar to those once worn by Russian peasant women.

A painted wooden horse from Poland

A recycled metal chameleon from Uganda

Painted wooden tigers from India

A terra-cotta clay leopard from Mexico

4

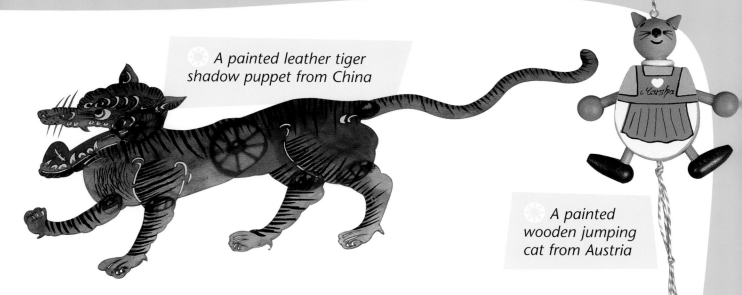

A painted leather tiger shadow puppet from China

A painted wooden jumping cat from Austria

A carved wooden car from India

Toys are usually made cheaply in factories or from whatever materials toymakers have available, such as scraps of wood, clay, leather, wire, cloth, or discarded tin cans.

This book explains how various toys and models have been designed. It also shows you how to make some of your own, using those from other places as a starting point.

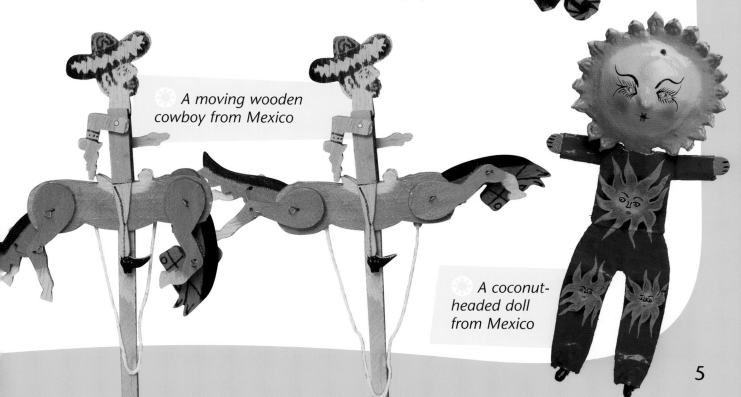

A moving wooden cowboy from Mexico

A coconut-headed doll from Mexico

Fanciful figures

Some craftspeople earn a living by making dolls to sell at fairs, either as toys for local children or as tourist souvenirs.

☀ This pair of musician dolls from the high Andes of Peru are dressed in typical warm, brightly colored woolen clothes and hats.

☀ Made from a single piece of turned wood, both these tiny Bengali dolls have painted features and clothes.

Look closer

- Both these skeletons have funny, animated expressions.

- The papier-mâché skeleton on the left is dressed as if she were alive, in an old-fashioned dress and hat, made from crêpe paper.

☀ Every November in Mexico, there is a festival called the Day of the Dead. People make model skeletons, like these, to display on the day.

Toy robots were first made in Japan after World War II and have become very popular. Unlike the two shown here, more sophisticated ones are powered by batteries.

Made from blocks of wood scraps, this Mexican robot has movable arms and legs.

Look closer

- Both robots have cube-shaped heads, but human features, such as eyes, a nose, and a mouth.

- They also have fake machine parts, such as dials, knobs, tubes, and antennae.

- The robots have been made so that their arms, legs, and head can move separately.

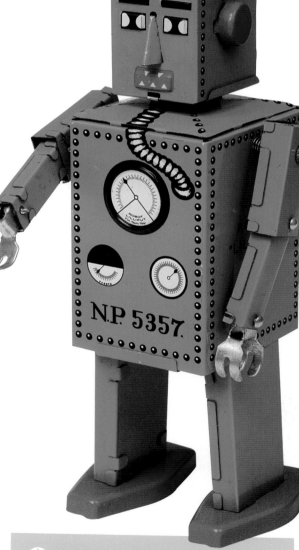
N.P. 5357.

This Chinese clockwork robot is made of painted metal. It walks when it is wound up.

Making a robot

You will need

- 10 cardboard boxes ● white glue
- paints and a paintbrush
- stickers ● 2 corks
- plastic bottle tops

Glue to make arm.

Glue to make arm.

1 Collect ten boxes the right size and shape for a robot's head, body, legs, feet, and arms. Glue the boxes for the head, body, legs, and feet together. Glue two small boxes together for each arm.

2 Paint all the robot parts the same color. Leave them to dry.

3 Paint two corks as antennae. Glue them on top of the robot's head.

4 Glue the arms onto the robot's body. Glue bottle caps on the head for eyes and ears.

Use stickers for the nose, mouth, and dials, or paint them on if you prefer.

Animal allsorts

Toymakers carve model animals from wood, sculpt them in paper pulp, wire, or metal, or create them from cloth.

Some toymakers make models of farm animals, such as cows, horses, and chickens. Even though their shapes are often quite simple and their colors unrealistic, the animals are still easily recognizable.

This hump-backed cow from India was made by covering a padded wooden frame with pieces of fabric.

This carved and decorated wooden horse is a traditional toy from Poland.

Paper-pulp cows like this are made as toys for village children in Bihar, India.

Look closer

Compare the way these three animals have been decorated.

- Each has a single background color.
- The decorations are brightly patterned in contrasting colors.
- The animals' features are extremely simple.

African craftspeople often make models of their wild animals. These are popular souvenirs for tourists who have been on a safari.

Cleverly sculpted from recycled sheet metal, this leopard from Uganda, with its ears pricked, looks ready to pounce on its prey.

Some toymakers prefer to make models of imaginary animals. Woodcarvers in Oaxaca, a town in Mexico, are famous for making winged horses and lizards, as well as two-headed birds, all painted in vivid colors.

Oaxacan carved animals are typically painted with a pattern of multicolored dots.

Making an animal

1 Model the head, body, and tail of an imaginary animal in self-hardening clay.

You will need

- a wooden board
- self-hardening clay
- paints and a paintbrush
- a bowl of water

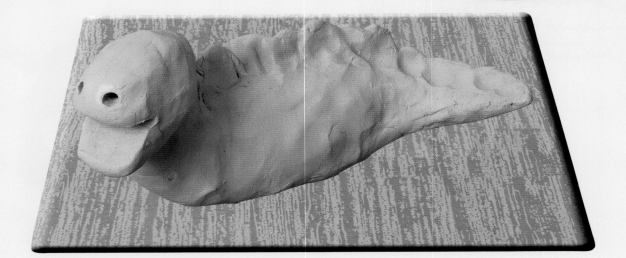

2 Model four sturdy legs. Attach them to the animal's body (see page 31).

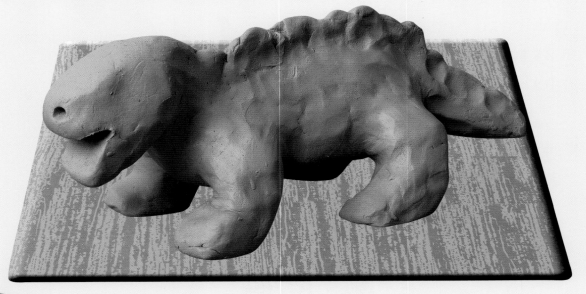

3 Model all sorts of features for your animal and fix them in place. Leave your model to dry completely.

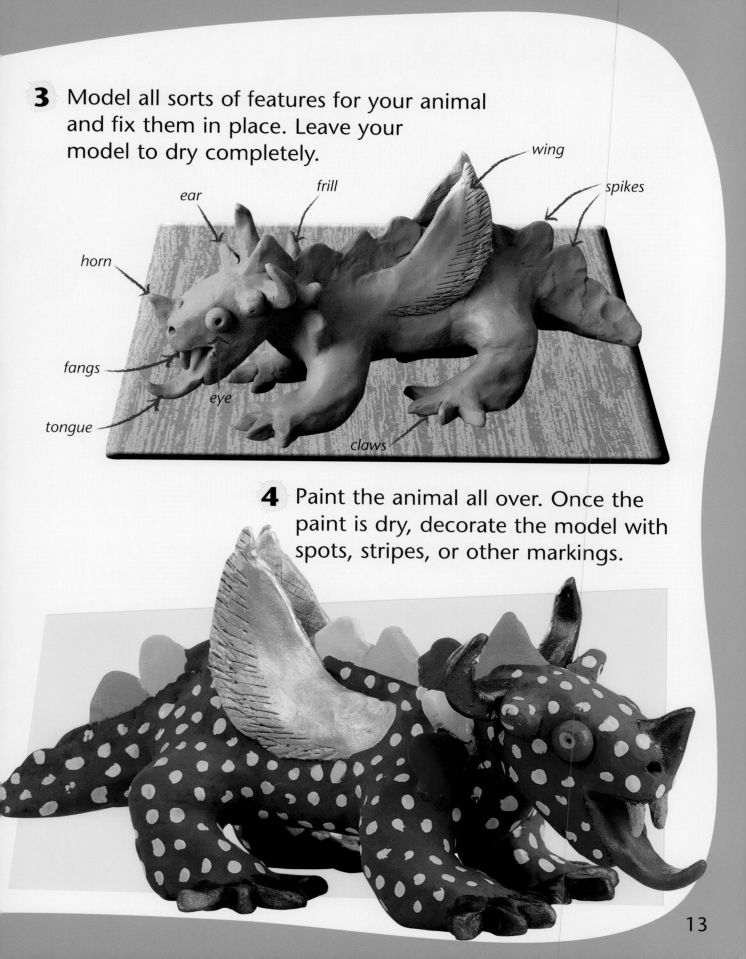

wing

frill

spikes

ear

horn

fangs

eye

tongue

claws

4 Paint the animal all over. Once the paint is dry, decorate the model with spots, stripes, or other markings.

Cars and trucks

Cars and trucks are favorite toys, especially if they can move. Many are accurate copies of real cars, including their design features, such as radiator grilles, markings, and logos.

This car froom India has been carved from soft wood and then stained.

This Mexican wooden truck is laden with real wood.

Look closer

- The wooden car *(above)* and truck *(left)* have wheels fixed to a rod (called an axle), so they can turn.

Made in Cuba from papier-mâché, this is a model of a 1951 Buick. Old American cars like this can still be seen on the streets of Cuba.

☀ *Made from recycled metal drinks cans in South Africa, this car is a model of a French 2CV.*

Look closer

- All these cars have been made from recycled metal.
- The wheels are painted bottle caps.
- The car parts have been soldered together.

☀ *This model Volkswagen car from the Ivory Coast has been entirely made from bent wire.*

☀ *In Madagascar, toymakers create model cars, such as this Citroën DS, from empty spray cans.*

Making a truck

1 Paint two boxes that are the right shape and size for a truck cab and trailer.

cab

trailer

wind deflector

2 Add details to the cab, such as a windshield, doors, lights, and a wind deflector. Glue or paint a picture on both sides of the trailer.

3 Pierce the center of eight bottle caps (see page 30). Make the holes big enough for a stick to fit through, as an axle.

4 Attach a wheel to each end of a skewer. Lay the stick across the trailer base. Push the wheels against the sides of the trailer. Snip off any extra skewer. Attach two sets of wheels onto the trailer and two onto the cab.

16

5 Cut two pieces of corrugated cardboard—one just smaller than the trailer base and the other just smaller than the cab base. Place them over the sticks and tape them in place.

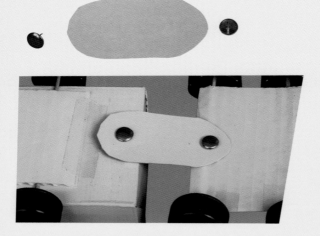

6 Cut out a small oval shape from the thin cardboard. Use thumbtacks to attach one end of the shape to the cab base and the other end to the base of the trailer, as shown.

17

Amusing action toys

Toymakers have invented all sorts of model people, who spring into action when they are pushed or pulled.

When the wooden handles are pushed, the Russian blacksmith and his bear helper take turns to beat an anvil with their hammers.

Look closer

- The blacksmith and the bear *(right)* are both carved from single pieces of wood.
- The fighters *(below)* have separate arms that can swing up and down.

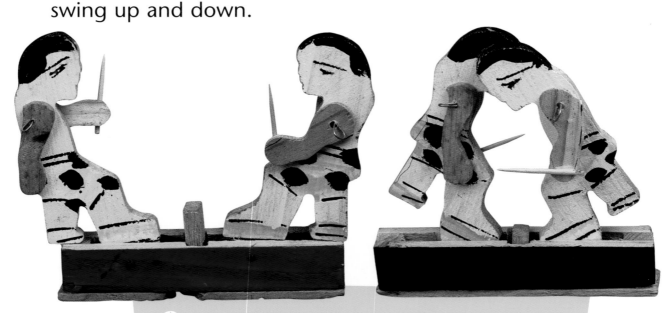

These two Mexican fighters wait with their swords raised. Both have one foot attached to a metal strip. When the wooden bar between them is pushed down, it bends the metal strip below, so that the fighters clash head to head.

When the string attached to this Mexican acrobat's hand is pulled, the acrobat leaps into the air and turns a somersault over the stick.

- Both toys on this page move by pulling a string.
- The limbs of both figures have all been made separately and then attached to the body.
- The legs of the acrobat *(left)* hang loose and swing up when the string is pulled.
- The arms and legs of the doll *(below)* are attached to the pulling string by another string, so that they all move at the same time.

This dancing doll from Austria is dressed in a traditional costume from the Tyrol, a mountainous region of the country.

Making an acrobat

You will need

- thin cardboard ● a pen or pencil ● scissors ● felt-tipped pens ● a pin ● a flat wooden stick ● thin, soft wire ● string

1 Draw the head and body, two legs and two arms of an acrobat on thin cardboard. Make one of the arms longer than the other.

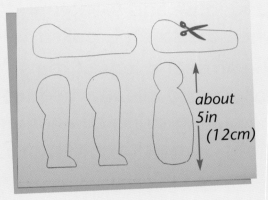

about 5in (12cm)

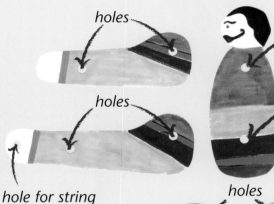

holes

hole for arms

holes

hole for legs

hole for string

holes

2 Cut out the pieces and color them in. Make holes in each piece in the places as shown (see page 30).

3 Push wire through the hole in one arm, the body, and the second arm. Twist the ends to hold the pieces in place. Do the same with the legs.

Make a hole near one end of the flat stick. Fit the arms on either side of the stick with wire.

4 Tie a piece of string through the hole at the end of the acrobat's longer arm. Pull the string and watch your acrobat somersault over the stick.

Animated animals

Many traditional wooden animal toys are made in separate parts. These are joined by string so the animals can be made to move in amusing, unexpected ways.

☼ *Made in Russia, this mother bear moves her arms up and down, so it looks as if she is washing her cub in the tub.*

☼ *This nodding tiger comes from Bangladesh. The carved wood has been painted with glowing details and then varnished.*

Look closer

- The tiger's body is in two parts, both firmly attached to a board. Its head and tail are fitted loosely between them.

- A ball is attached by string to the head and tail. When the ball is swung, these jointed parts move up and down.

- The chickens have separate heads attached to a string. The strings are attached to a ball.

- When the ball is swung, the chickens' heads bob up and down.

- Their beaks peck noisily against the grain painted on the board.

✺ *Pecking chickens are a traditional Russian toy.*

These two toys are made from large and small beads, strung onto elastic, which is attached to a flat plate underneath. When the plate is pushed up, the toys move in different directions.

✺ *Comical wooden animals, like these, are made and hand-painted in the Czech Republic.*

23

Making a nodding tiger

You will need adult help with this project.

You will need

- thin white cardboard ● a pencil
- scissors ● paints and a paintbrush ● toothpicks
- a large bead ● strong thread
- 2 pins

1 Draw the head, body, and tail of a tiger on thin cardboard. Cut them out. Cut a second body, using the first one as a guide.

Cut four small rectangles, and a base large enough for your tiger to stand on.

head   tail

rectangles   tiger's body

base

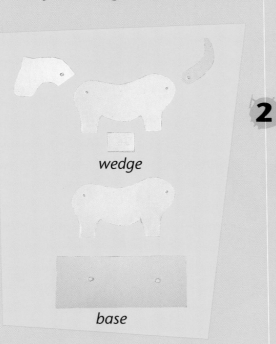

wedge

base

2 Make holes in the body pieces, as shown, small enough for a toothpick to fit in tightly.

Make larger holes in the head and tail, so that the toothpick fits through these loosely.

Make two big holes in the base—in line with the tiger's legs.

3 Glue the four cardboard rectangles together to make a wedge. Paint the tiger pieces, the wedge, and the base.

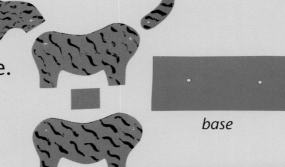

base

4 Glue the wedge in the center, between the two body pieces. Tape the tiger's legs to the base.

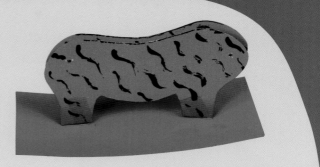

5 Cut 20in (50cm) of strong thread. Fold it in half. Push the looped end through the bead and tie a knot (see page 30). Tie a pin to each loose end.

6 Thread each pin through a hole in the base and between the body pieces. Push one pin into the tiger's head and the other into the tail.

7 Fit the head between the body pieces. Push a toothpick through the front holes to keep it in place. Trim the ends of the stick. Do the same with the tail.

Swing or pull the bead to make your tiger move.

Playful puppets

Children play with puppets. People also use puppets to perform plays, often during festivals.

Hand puppets fit over your hand. String puppets have jointed parts, each attached to its own string so that it can be moved separately. Shadow puppets are flat and have holes to let light through. Puppeteers perform with them from behind a backlit white cloth screen.

✺ Created in Bangladesh, these hand puppets are made from jute. Their clothes, hair, and features have been sewn on.

✺ The wooden head of this Austrian cloth puppet is attached to the top of a stick. When the stick is pushed up through the cardboard cone, the puppet pops up.

This Mexican horse puppet is made from papier-mâché.

Look closer

- The legs of the string puppets *(above)* and the shadow puppet *(below)* are hinged, which allows them to move in all sorts of ways.

- The elephant's head is joined to its body with a circle of leather so that it can be turned.

Separate strings are attached to this Thai wooden puppet's head, body, and trunk. The trunk is jointed, so it can twist. The ears can flap. The cloth tail twitches when the string on the body is pulled.

This Indian leather shadow puppet has been inked with strong black lines and markings, so that these show up on the screen.

Making a puppet

1 Draw the head, body, and hands of a hand puppet on some thin white cardboard. Make sure the shape is bigger than your hand. Cut it out.

You will need

● thin white cardboard ● pieces of felt in different colors ● scissors ● a pen ● pins ● fabric glue ● a needle and thread

2 Pin the cardboard puppet to a piece of felt. Then cut around it.

3 Cut out a second felt shape, using the cardboard shape as a cutting guide.

4 Cut out some clothes, hair, eyes, and a mouth from pieces of felt in contrasting colors.

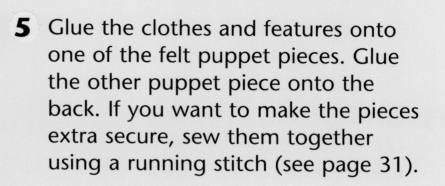

5 Glue the clothes and features onto one of the felt puppet pieces. Glue the other puppet piece onto the back. If you want to make the pieces extra secure, sew them together using a running stitch (see page 31).

Handy hints

Making holes

1 To make a hole in a plastic bottle cap, press the cap upside-down on top of a ball of soft modeling clay.

2 Pierce the center of the cap with a sharp tool, such as a bradawl or closed scissor tips.

To make a hole in a piece of thin cardboard, set the card on top of some modeling clay and push a thumbtack in where you want a hole to be.

Tying a reef knot

1 Tie one end of a piece of string from right to left over and under the second end.

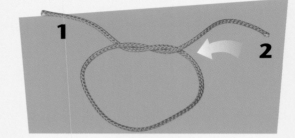

2 Now tie the first end of string from *left* to *right* over and under the second end.

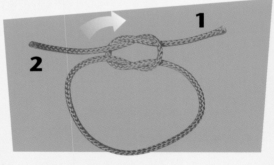

3 Pull the two ends to make a tight knot.

Running stitch

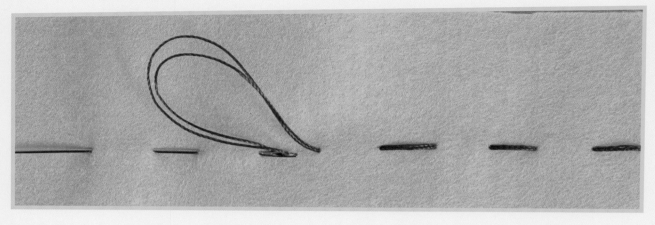

Thread a needle. Knot both ends of the thread together. Push the needle in and out of the fabric.

Keep the stitches and spaces small and even. Finish off by sewing a couple of stitches on top of each other.

Joining clay pieces together

1 Using a blunt knife, crisscross the two pieces of clay where you want to join them.

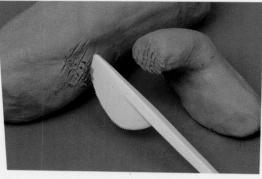

2 Wet the crisscrossed areas with water.

3 Push the two pieces of clay firmly together. Smooth the join with your finger.

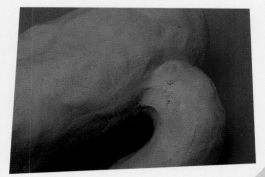

Glossary

backlit lit from behind

bradawl a small tool with a point for making holes

jute a plant with long fibrous leaves, used for making sacks and rugs

paper pulp paper that has been soaked and softened into a soggy mass

robot a machine that can do things like a person

recycled not made from new materials, but from an object or material that has been saved and used again

solder to join two pieces of metal with some melted metal

Index